52 Lessons Every Father Must Teach His Son

Corey Pruitt

ISBN: 0692211063
ISBN-13: 978-0692211069

DEDICATION

This book is dedicated to:

My Step-Father – Dave
For passing on many of these life lessons to me.

My three sons – Zach, Riley and Aiden
For being open to learning and growing.

CONTENTS

CHAPTER 1

WHY

Why this book? Why now? These are two questions you may be asking yourself right at this moment. Well, the short answer is, because it is time.

All of us, Fathers, are daily living in the balancing act of life. Balancing mounting work obligations with growing family obligations... balancing hours... balancing finances... balancing relationships... balancing chores... and on, and on.

We live in a busy time of life!

Even though we star in this balancing act, as men we still have a desire to add more to our "show." Our thinking is that more for a little while may equal less time and resource investment in the long run. And, at times, we may be right. Or, our thinking is, this time investment is worth it in the end.

When it comes to the purpose of this book, absolutely, this time and resource investment in your son is worth it. The return on your time investment is greater than any stock market return, or business deal. The return on your investment is the integrity and success of your son.

What this book is not...
This book is not going to help you by sharing three strategies for managing your work load. Or share seven fool-proof ways to bring happiness to your relationships. This book isn't even going to share with you the elusive secrets of time management.

What this book is...

This book is your game plan for how you can impact your son's life.

Stew on this crazy thought. At work you have project plans, goal sessions and work lists. When you exercise you follow a workout plan or routine. In your finances you have a budget, saving and spending plans. You have retirement plans... business plans... lesson plans... you have meal plans... heck, you probably even have weekend plans!

In all these areas of our lives we have taken some level of calculated effort to reach a pre-defined idea or goal. And, this is a great thing! This is how we, as men and Fathers, manage all that is required of us. But, for some reason we leave the integrity and success of our sons to chance.

> *If one does not know to which port one is sailing, no wind is favorable.*
> *Lucius Annaeus Seneca*

For some reason, along the path of life, we made the collective decision (often subconsciously) to allow others to lead our sons; others such as, coaches, teachers, media, their mom, their friends, their friends' parents, etc. Or, sadly, many sons are having to lead themselves and that "self-taught standard" is often lower than if someone else more experienced would have done the leading.

So, you see, the time is now. The time is now for us to make a calculated effort toward the integrity and success of our sons. The time is now for us to follow a simple game plan that will yield enormous results.

"The pages in this book have the potential to positively impact the life of your son, and your relationship with your son."

The 52 lessons that follow are lessons that will impact your son on multiple levels. They are lessons that can be learned and reinforced no matter the age of your son. And, they are lessons that are best taught by a Father or Father-Figure.

CHAPTER 2

HOW

***Don't wait for extraordinary opportunities. Seize
common occasions and make them great.***
Orison Swett Marden

This book is designed for you to focus on one lesson
per week for a year. On the left page you will see the life
lesson. On the right page you will see three questions with
space to write your thoughts.

- Question #1: How can I best teach my son this
  lesson?
- Question #2: Now that I have taught my son this
  lesson, how can I best reinforce this lesson?
- Question #3: If I were to teach it again, what
  would I do differently?

These questions are meant to get your "fatherly juices"
flowing about the best way to pass the lesson along to your
son. It is not a lengthy, let's-form-a-committee-and-
analyze-this-to-death, process. Rather it is a quick, but
calculated, decision process.

Let's unpack these questions a little more, to provide
some direction.

Q1: How can I best teach my son this lesson?
There are a million ways to teach your son. Think
about how you might best be able to share this lesson with
him. Is it while:
- Playing video games with him...
- Watching sports...

- Playing sports...
- Putting a Lego structure together...
- Out for a special father and son breakfast...
- Sipping on a smoothie or coffee...

Is this lesson better suited for a:
- Face to face conversation (which should be your default)
- Through a phone call
- Through a letter or email

Can you share this lesson through:
- A direct conversation...
- A story about your life that perfectly depicts the lesson...
- A high profile example currently in the Media...
- An example of something that happened to him in the past...
- An example of how he could have dealt with something differently...
- A story about one of his friends or a peer he looks up to...

What type of learner is your son? Is your son more of a
- Visual learner... (show him something)
- Active learner with his body... (have him experience something)
- Auditory learner... (tell him something)

Q2: Now that I have taught my son this, how can I best reinforce this lesson?

Your second question is all about reinforcement. Most lessons will need a little reinforcement. These life lessons are often not a one pop deal. So begin to think about how might you go about reinforcing this lesson in the upcoming weeks?

Also, begin to think about how you might check to see that your son caught what you were throwing?

Q3: If I were to teach it again, what would I do differently?

This last question is your time to reflect on what was successful and what bombed. We can spend a lot of time talking about "the big game" and the "dropped passes" on Monday morning, but spend little time reflecting on how the "big game" of being a Father is paying out.

So, think of yourself as the "Monday morning quarterback" of your son's success, and reflect on how the lessons are going. What's working? What's not working? What metaphorical balls were dropped by you? What one's were dropped by your son? What "passes" of yours just did not hit the mark? And, what passes of yours were right on target.

> *A person who never made a mistake*
> *never tried anything new.*
> *Albert Einstein*

This reflection process is critical to the success of your future lessons, so don't skip this piece of the process.

Jump in...

Well, what are you waiting for? It is time to get started. Don't delay. Don't drag your feet. Don't come up with excuses as to why you can't start now. It all comes down to jumping in!

> *You can have results or excuses,*
> *you can't have both.*
> *Anonymous*

You are not going to get it right every time. You will fumble some weeks, but that is okay. Your son is not looking for a polished presentation with corresponding PowerPoint slides. Your son is not expecting a sophisticated and refined sales pitch. Your son is not even looking for anything remotely close to perfection.

Besides, the worst that can happen is you have an awkward moment with your son every once in a while throughout the year...I guarantee your son would take awkward moments with you over no moments with you, any day!

There are no secrets to success. It is the result of preparation, hard work, and learning from failure.
Colin Powell

So, jump in!

Corey Pruitt

CHAPTER 3

THE LESSONS

1
Teach him to laugh

How can I best teach my son this lesson?

Now that I have taught my son this lesson, how can I best reinforce this lesson?

If I were to teach it again, what would I do differently?

2
Teach him the importance of having his money work for him

How can I best teach my son this lesson?

Now that I have taught my son this lesson, how can I best reinforce this lesson?

If I were to teach it again, what would I do differently?

3

Teach him to show honor and respect toward women

How can I best teach my son this lesson?

Now that I have taught my son this lesson, how can I best reinforce this lesson?

If I were to teach it again, what would I do differently?

4

Teach him not to fight, but to confront and defend with grace

How can I best teach my son this lesson?

Now that I have taught my son this lesson, how can I best reinforce this lesson?

If I were to teach it again, what would I do differently?

5

Teach him how to pray

How can I best teach my son this lesson?

Now that I have taught my son this lesson, how can I best reinforce this lesson?

If I were to teach it again, what would I do differently?

6

Teach him how to respect his mom

How can I best teach my son this lesson?

Now that I have taught my son this lesson, how can I best reinforce this lesson?

If I were to teach it again, what would I do differently?

7

Teach him no one ever makes him do, feel, say or think anything…he always has a choice

How can I best teach my son this lesson?

Now that I have taught my son this lesson, how can I best reinforce this lesson?

If I were to teach it again, what would I do differently?

8

Teach him to respect himself

How can I best teach my son this lesson?

Now that I have taught my son this lesson, how can I best reinforce this lesson?

If I were to teach it again, what would I do differently?

9

Teach him that it is ok to tell people he loves them
(tell him you love him over and over again...forever)

How can I best teach my son this lesson?

Now that I have taught my son this lesson, how can I best reinforce this lesson?

If I were to teach it again, what would I do differently?

10

Teach him the importance of family

How can I best teach my son this lesson?

Now that I have taught my son this lesson, how can I best reinforce this lesson?

If I were to teach it again, what would I do differently?

11

Teach him to have passion about life

How can I best teach my son this lesson?

Now that I have taught my son this lesson, how can I best reinforce this lesson?

If I were to teach it again, what would I do differently?

12

Teach him that it is ok to have feelings like sad, hurt, angry, happy, love, excitement…and teach him how to positively express those feelings

How can I best teach my son this lesson?

Now that I have taught my son this lesson, how can I best reinforce this lesson?

If I were to teach it again, what would I do differently?

13

Teach him to pick his friends wisely

How can I best teach my son this lesson?

Now that I have taught my son this lesson, how can I best reinforce this lesson?

If I were to teach it again, what would I do differently?

14

Teach him that life is not always fair

How can I best teach my son this lesson?

Now that I have taught my son this lesson, how can I best reinforce this lesson?

If I were to teach it again, what would I do differently?

15

Teach him that expressing himself with well-chosen words always has a better result

How can I best teach my son this lesson?

Now that I have taught my son this lesson, how can I best reinforce this lesson?

If I were to teach it again, what would I do differently?

16

Teach him about faith

How can I best teach my son this lesson?

Now that I have taught my son this lesson, how can I best reinforce this lesson?

If I were to teach it again, what would I do differently?

17

Teach him about the benefits of working hard

How can I best teach my son this lesson?

Now that I have taught my son this lesson, how can I best reinforce this lesson?

If I were to teach it again, what would I do differently?

18

Teach him to be trustworthy and straightforward

How can I best teach my son this lesson?

Now that I have taught my son this lesson, how can I best reinforce this lesson?

If I were to teach it again, what would I do differently?

19

Teach him to make decisions with the future in mind

How can I best teach my son this lesson?

Now that I have taught my son this lesson, how can I best reinforce this lesson?

If I were to teach it again, what would I do differently?

20

Teach him to teach himself

How can I best teach my son this lesson?

Now that I have taught my son this lesson, how can I best reinforce this lesson?

If I were to teach it again, what would I do differently?

21

Teach him the importance of keeping his word

How can I best teach my son this lesson?

Now that I have taught my son this lesson, how can I best reinforce this lesson?

If I were to teach it again, what would I do differently?

22

Teach him about the power in complimenting others

How can I best teach my son this lesson?

Now that I have taught my son this lesson, how can I best reinforce this lesson?

If I were to teach it again, what would I do differently?

23

Teach him not to quit out of frustration

How can I best teach my son this lesson?

Now that I have taught my son this lesson, how can I best reinforce this lesson?

If I were to teach it again, what would I do differently?

24

Teach him to clean up after himself

How can I best teach my son this lesson?

Now that I have taught my son this lesson, how can I best reinforce this lesson?

If I were to teach it again, what would I do differently?

25

Teach him to be a giver

How can I best teach my son this lesson?

Now that I have taught my son this lesson, how can I best reinforce this lesson?

If I were to teach it again, what would I do differently?

26

Teach him to respect all people regardless of position, gender or color

How can I best teach my son this lesson?

Now that I have taught my son this lesson, how can I best reinforce this lesson?

If I were to teach it again, what would I do differently?

27

Teach him to always give 100% in everything he does

How can I best teach my son this lesson?

Now that I have taught my son this lesson, how can I best reinforce this lesson?

If I were to teach it again, what would I do differently?

28

Teach him to never be afraid to try new things

How can I best teach my son this lesson?

Now that I have taught my son this lesson, how can I best reinforce this lesson?

If I were to teach it again, what would I do differently?

29

Teach him to celebrate victories and to learn from defeats

How can I best teach my son this lesson?

Now that I have taught my son this lesson, how can I best reinforce this lesson?

If I were to teach it again, what would I do differently?

30

Teach him the importance of exercise

How can I best teach my son this lesson?

Now that I have taught my son this lesson, how can I best reinforce this lesson?

If I were to teach it again, what would I do differently?

31

Teach him not to criticize others

How can I best teach my son this lesson?

Now that I have taught my son this lesson, how can I best reinforce this lesson?

If I were to teach it again, what would I do differently?

32

Teach him that you will always be his biggest fan

How can I best teach my son this lesson?

Now that I have taught my son this lesson, how can I best reinforce this lesson?

If I were to teach it again, what would I do differently?

33

Teach him to practice patience

How can I best teach my son this lesson?

Now that I have taught my son this lesson, how can I best reinforce this lesson?

If I were to teach it again, what would I do differently?

34

Teach him how to lose and how to win with humility

How can I best teach my son this lesson?

Now that I have taught my son this lesson, how can I best reinforce this lesson?

If I were to teach it again, what would I do differently?

35

Teach him that self-worth does not come through the approval of his peers

How can I best teach my son this lesson?

Now that I have taught my son this lesson, how can I best reinforce this lesson?

If I were to teach it again, what would I do differently?

36

Teach him to forgive, because harboring wrongs is no way to live

How can I best teach my son this lesson?

Now that I have taught my son this lesson, how can I best reinforce this lesson?

If I were to teach it again, what would I do differently?

37

Teach him to set goals and how to reach them

How can I best teach my son this lesson?

Now that I have taught my son this lesson, how can I best reinforce this lesson?

If I were to teach it again, what would I do differently?

38

Teach him about moderation

How can I best teach my son this lesson?

Now that I have taught my son this lesson, how can I best reinforce this lesson?

If I were to teach it again, what would I do differently?

39

Teach him to be accountable for his decisions and actions

How can I best teach my son this lesson?

Now that I have taught my son this lesson, how can I best reinforce this lesson?

If I were to teach it again, what would I do differently?

40

Teach him how to work for what he really wants

How can I best teach my son this lesson?

Now that I have taught my son this lesson, how can I best reinforce this lesson?

If I were to teach it again, what would I do differently?

41

Teach him to be humble

How can I best teach my son this lesson?

Now that I have taught my son this lesson, how can I best reinforce this lesson?

If I were to teach it again, what would I do differently?

42

Teach him to have big dreams

How can I best teach my son this lesson?

Now that I have taught my son this lesson, how can I best reinforce this lesson?

If I were to teach it again, what would I do differently?

43

Teach him that God answers prayer

How can I best teach my son this lesson?

Now that I have taught my son this lesson, how can I best reinforce this lesson?

If I were to teach it again, what would I do differently?

44

Teach him to keep commitments

How can I best teach my son this lesson?

Now that I have taught my son this lesson, how can I best reinforce this lesson?

If I were to teach it again, what would I do differently?

45

Teach him that his thoughts will determine his actions and attitudes

How can I best teach my son this lesson?

Now that I have taught my son this lesson, how can I best reinforce this lesson?

If I were to teach it again, what would I do differently?

46

Teach him that he is capable to accomplish anything

How can I best teach my son this lesson?

Now that I have taught my son this lesson, how can I best reinforce this lesson?

If I were to teach it again, what would I do differently?

47

Teach him about Jesus

How can I best teach my son this lesson?

Now that I have taught my son this lesson, how can I best reinforce this lesson?

If I were to teach it again, what would I do differently?

48

Teach him the words
"impossible" and "never" are
not a part of his vocabulary

How can I best teach my son this lesson?

Now that I have taught my son this lesson, how can I best reinforce this lesson?

If I were to teach it again, what would I do differently?

49

Teach him that preparation + determination = success

How can I best teach my son this lesson?

Now that I have taught my son this lesson, how can I best reinforce this lesson?

If I were to teach it again, what would I do differently?

50

Teach him there is no value in jealousy, but great value in thankfulness

How can I best teach my son this lesson?

Now that I have taught my son this lesson, how can I best reinforce this lesson?

If I were to teach it again, what would I do differently?

51

Teach him that what he feeds his thoughts is what he will get in return

How can I best teach my son this lesson?

Now that I have taught my son this lesson, how can I best reinforce this lesson?

If I were to teach it again, what would I do differently?

52

Teach him that, even though he is good at something, there is always room to improve

How can I best teach my son this lesson?

Now that I have taught my son this lesson, how can I best reinforce this lesson?

If I were to teach it again, what would I do differently?

CHAPTER 4

WHAT NOW?

Well, what now? Wash, rinse, repeat! Start back at lesson one and do it all over again. Read what you wrote for your questions #2 and #3. Make changes as necessary... and... enjoy the journey!

ABOUT THE AUTHOR

Corey is most proud of being a father of 4 kids (three sons and a daughter). He is a self-proclaimed "Father in training" as he learns on the job.

Corey is a thought leader and innovator specializing in professional and personal development, strategic communication, motivation and performance improvement.

He is a highly motivated, nationally known speaker and trainer. He has a keen ability to inspire new learning, facilitate new actions and impact change. His work transforms both people and businesses.

Corey draws from his experience as a Counselor, Business Owner, Motivation and Performance Trainer, Communication and Psychology Professor, and various leadership positions in higher education.

To get more information about Corey or other information, connect at www.ChangeSparx.com.

Made in the USA
Coppell, TX
06 January 2024

27367356R00069